ELIE WIESEL
Messenger from the Holocaust

by Carol Greene

CHILDRENS PRESS, CHICAGO®

PICTURE ACKNOWLEDGMENTS:

Wide World Photos, Inc.—Cover, 1, 3, 5, 10, 13 (2 photos), 14, 15 (top), 17, 18, 19 (left), 21, 22, 24, 25, 26, 27, 32
United Press International—6, 8
Historical Pictures Service, Chicago—7
National Archives—11 (2 photos), 12, 20
Photri—15 (bottom)
U.S. Army Photograph—16, 19 (right)
Spertus Museum of Judaica—29
Cover—Elie Wiesel

Library of Congress Cataloging-in-Publication Data

Greene, Carol.
    Elie Wiesel, messenger from the Holocaust.

    Summary: A brief biography of the winner of the 1986 Nobel Peace Prize, who having survived the Holocaust, dedicated his life to speaking and writing about these terrible events so that they would not be forgotten.
    1. Wiesel, Elie, 1928-   —Biography—Juvenile literature.   2.   Authors, French—20th century—Biography—Juvenile literature.   3.   Holocaust, Jewish (1939-1945)—Juvenile literature.   [1.   Wiesel, Elie, 1928
2.   Authors, French.   3.   Holocaust, Jewish (1939-1945)]
I.   Title.
PQ2683.I32Z687   1987   813'.54   [B] [92]   87-6341
ISBN 0-516-03490-1

Elie Wiesel receives an honorary degree from the University
of Hartford, June 5, 1985.

On Monday, October 13, 1986, Elie Wiesel went to the Fifth Avenue Synagogue in New York City. It was Yom Kippur, the most holy day in the Jewish year. With other Jews, Wiesel fasted and prayed.

On his way home, a newspaper reporter stopped him. Wiesel was going to win the Nobel Peace Prize, the reporter said. His paper wanted to do a story about it. Elie Wiesel did not believe him. He told the reporter that his paper was wrong.

But at five o'clock the next morning, the Wiesels' telephone rang. It was a long-distance call from Oslo, Norway. Jakob Sverdrup, Director of the Nobel Institute, told Elie Wiesel that he *had* won the Nobel Peace Prize.

At eleven o'clock, the Nobel Committee announced the news to

the rest of the world. After that, the
Wiesels' phone didn't stop ringing.
Everyone wanted to congratulate
Elie Wiesel. The President of France
couldn't even get through.

For his peace efforts, Elie Wiesel receives the 1986 Nobel
Peace Prize. Standing behind him is his son, Shlomo Elisha.

What did Elie Wiesel do to win
the Nobel Peace Prize? Why were so
many people glad that he did win it?

Elie Wiesel remembered what
happened to Jewish people during
World War II. He remembered—and
he told stories.

His own story began in Sighet, a
town in the Carpathian Mountains.

6

Today it is part of Rumania. Eliezer Wiesel was born there on September 30, 1928.

His parents, Shlomo and Sarah, ran a shop. His older sisters, Hilda and Batya, helped them. Later, a little sister, Tzipora, was born.

Elie's job, said his family, was to go to school. He learned to read and

write. He studied Hebrew, the Torah, the Talmud, and the works of other Jewish writers. He even studied the violin with a police captain.

Elie loved to learn, especially about his religion. Sometimes, it

seemed as if he just couldn't learn enough. There were other Jewish writers he wanted to study. But who could teach him?

That was when he made friends with Moshe. Moshe was a poor man who worked around the synagogue. He knew about those other Jewish writers. So he helped Elie.

But Elie had another teacher, too. His grandfather Dodye Feig lived on a farm. There, Elie could eat apricots, apples, and plums off the trees. He could watch Dodye Feig tend the cows and till the fields.

Sometimes, when the day was over, Dodye Feig told Elie old Jewish stories. Sometimes, he sang old songs. And sometimes, the two just sat quietly and watched the evening turn into night.

Adolf Hitler (above) was responsible for the deaths of six million Jewish people.

All that ended in the spring of 1944. At that time, many countries were fighting World War II. The German leader, Adolf Hitler, and his Nazis had a dreadful plan. Everyone should be like them, they thought. Then the world would be a better place. Jews were not like them. So they would kill all the Jews in the countries they controlled.

During Nazi rule German children were taught to believe that Jews were their enemies. It was an honor to die for Germany in the battle to make their people the master race.

Jews, hands raised, were cruelly taken from their homes and marched to waiting trains.

Fifteen thousand Jewish people lived in Sighet. They were all put on cattle trains and taken to a concentration camp in Poland. The camp's name was Auschwitz.

Elie and his family got off the train with the others. "Men to the left! Women to the right!" ordered a Nazi guard.

Prisoners arrive at Auschwitz (above), a Nazi death camp.
Men, women, and children lived separately. These women
(below) wait for their work assignment.

Elie held his father's hand. They must stay together. He watched his mother and sisters move away. He never saw his mother or little Tzipora again. They were killed at Auschwitz. Hilda and Batya did not die. But Elie did not know that until much later.

Months went by. Elie and his father had to do heavy work. They had very little food. Sometimes, the guards beat them. Many of the people with them were killed. They knew they might be killed, too.

Today fresh flowers are placed daily on transport cars that once carried bodies to the ovens at Auschwitz to be burned.

Two and a half million people were executed at Auschwitz.
A half million died of starvation. Often hundreds of bodies
were left unburied.

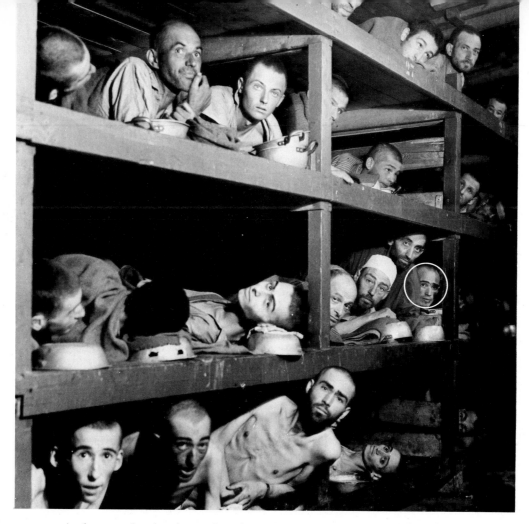

A photograph taken by an American Army photographer in April 1945 shows Elie Wiesel (circled) in the Buchenwald camp.

In January of 1945, the Nazis moved them to another concentration camp called Buchenwald. There, Elie's father died of disease and starvation. Now Elie was truly alone.

On April 11, 1945, an American tank pulled up at Buchenwald. At last, the prisoners were free. But where could Elie go? His parents were dead. He had no one left in Sighet.

After the camp was captured by American troops, children were taken to an American hospital for treatment. Few had homes or families to take care of them.

He ended up in Paris, France. He learned French and studied at the Sorbonne, a university there. To earn a living, he led a choir, taught the Bible and Hebrew, worked at a summer camp, and did translations.

The Sorbonne (below) was once one of the best European schools for the study of Theology.

Children freed from the Buchenwald prison camp (left) still manage to smile. Although broken and starving, they escaped death. Millions were not as fortunate. Their bodies were burned or buried in common graves.

Elie knew now that the Nazis had killed six million Jewish people. One million of them were children. He had seen many of these people die. Their stories crowded his mind. He knew that someday he must tell these stories. He had "to give testimony, to bear witness."

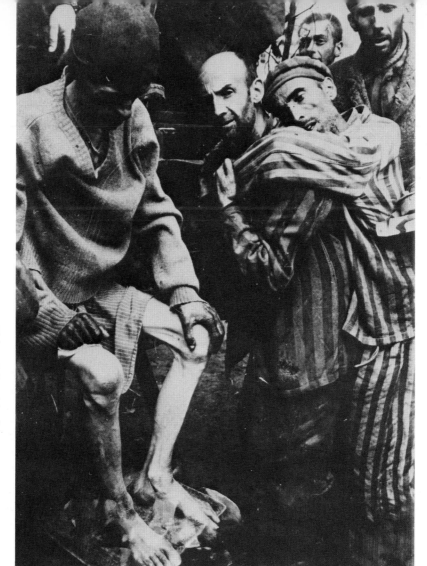

Elie Wiesel and other survivors of Nazi concentration camps would carry the memories and the suffering of this time all of their lives.

But not yet. The stories were too precious, too important. What had happened was too terrible. "I didn't want to use the wrong words," he explained. So he decided to wait for ten years.

Meanwhile, he became a journalist. He worked first for a French paper, then for an Israeli one. In 1954, the Israeli paper sent him to interview the French writer, François Mauriac.

François Mauriac received the Nobel Peace Prize in 1952 for his religious writings.

Something special happened at that meeting. Elie began to talk about himself. He told Mauriac some of the stories that lived inside him. Mauriac just listened. He couldn't say a word. When Elie finished, the old man put his arms around him and cried.

But Mauriac knew what Elie must do. He must wait no longer. He must tell those stories to the world.

Author Wiesel holds the first printing of his writings entitled Against Silence.

So Elie began. His first book was very long. It was published in South America in 1956. In 1958, Elie published a much shorter version in France. Its English title is *Night*. The dedication reads: "In memory of my parents and of my little sister Tzipora."

After *Night,* Elie Wiesel wrote many books. Some of them are: *Dawn, The Accident, The Town beyond the Wall, The Gates of the Forest,* and *A Beggar in Jerusalem.* He was the first to use the word "holocaust" for what had happened to the Jews.

In 1956, Elie Wiesel was hit by a taxi in New York City. He had to stay in a wheelchair for a year. During that time, he decided to become a United States citizen.

Accepting the Congressional gold medal from President Reagan, April 19, 1985

"I'm grateful to America," he said later. But that does not stop him from speaking up when he thinks his country is doing something wrong. In 1985, he told President Ronald Reagan that he should not visit a Nazi cemetery in Germany. He has also spoken up for suffering people in Cambodia, South Africa, Honduras, the Middle East, and other places.

He made several trips to the Soviet Union and saw that Jews still suffered there. So he began to tell their stories, too. *The Jews of Silence* and *The Testament* are two of his books about Soviet Jews.

In 1969, Elie Wiesel married Marian Erster Rose. She had also been in a concentration camp. They have one son, called Shlomo after Elie's father. Mrs. Wiesel also has a daughter, Jennifer, from an earlier marriage.

Elie with his wife and son after a New York news conference

The Wiesels live in New York City. There, Elie gives lectures and writes—in French. Some of his later stories are about the old Jewish writers and teachers he loved as a child. He also travels to Boston, where he is on the faculty of Boston University. Marian translates his writings into English.

Wiesel is greeted by the president of Hartford University after being awarded the honorary degree of Doctor of Humanities.

Speaking at the White House in 1979 as chairman of President Carter's Holocaust Committee

Elie Wiesel has won many prizes for his work. Some of them are: the Eleanor Roosevelt Award, the Martin Luther King Medallion, the Frank and Ethel Cohen Award, the Jewish Book Council Literary Award, the Congressional Gold Medal of Achievement, and several French awards.

In 1978, President Jimmy Carter made him chairman of the United States Holocaust Memorial Council.

That council has two jobs. One is to help people remember those who died in the Nazi Holocaust. The other is the help people learn that there must never be another holocaust.

On April 24, 1979, Elie Wiesel gave a speech at the U.S. Capitol in Washington, D.C.

"Let us remember for their sakes, and ours," he said. "Memory may perhaps be our only answer, our only hope to save the world from the ultimate punishment, a nuclear holocaust."

When that phone call from Norway told him about the Nobel Peace Prize, Elie Wiesel said he was "very stunned and grateful." But then he did what he has always done. He remembered. Before any celebrating started, he thought about his parents and grandparents.

Later, he said that the $270,000 cash part of the prize would let him "speak louder" and "reach more people."

"I owe something to the dead," he said. "...Anyone who does not remember betrays them again."

Because of Elie Wiesel, people all over the world have heard stories of those who died. And they remember.

WIESEL'S SPEECH:

Following is the prepared text of the acceptance speech by Elie Wiesel, the winner of the 1986 Nobel Peace Prize:

It is with a profound sense of humility that I accept the honor you have chosen to bestow upon me. I know: your choice transcends me. This both frightens and pleases me.

It pleases me because I wonder: do I have the right to represent the multitudes who have perished? Do I have the right to accept this great honor on their behalf? I do not. That would be presumptuous. No one may speak for the dead, no one may interpret their mutilated dreams and visions.

It pleases me because I may say that this honor belongs to all the survivors and their children, and through us, to the Jewish people with whose destiny I have always identified.

I remember: it happened yesterday or eternities ago. A young Jewish boy discovered the kingdom of night. I remember his bewilderment, I remember his anguish. It all happened so fast. The ghetto. The deportation. The sealed cattle car. The fiery altar upon which the history of our people and the future of mankind were meant to be sacrificed.

'Can This Be True?'

I remember: he asked his father: "Can this be true? This is the 20th century, not the Middle Ages. Who would allow such crimes to be committed? How could the world remain silent?"

And now the boy is turning to me: "Tell me," he asks. "What have you done with my future? What have you done with your life?"

And I tell him that I have tried. That I have tried to keep memory alive, that I have tried to fight those who would forget. Because if we forget, we are guilty, we are accomplices.

And then I explained to him how naive we were, that the world did know and remain silent. And that is why I swore never to be silent whenever and wherever human beings endure suffering and humiliation. We must always take sides. Neutrality helps the oppressor, never the victim. Silence encourages the tormentor, never the tormented.

'Sometimes We Must Interfere'

Sometimes we must interfere. When human lives are endangered, when human dignity is in jeopardy, national borders and sensitivities become irrelevant. Wherever men or women are persecuted because of their race, religion or political views, that place must—at that moment —become the center of the universe.

Of course, since I am a Jew profoundly rooted in my people's memory and tradition, my first response is to Jewish fears, Jewish needs, Jewish crises. For I belong to a traumatized generation, one that experienced the abandonment and

'This Honor Belongs to All the Survivors'

solitude of our people. It would be unnatural for me not to make Jewish priorities my own: Israel, Soviet Jewry, Jews in Arab lands.

But there are others as important to me. Apartheid is, in my view, as abhorrent as anti-Semitism. To me, Andrei Sakharov's isolation is as much of a disgrace as Iosif Begun's imprisonment. As is the denial of Solidarity and its leader Lech Walesa's right to dissent. And Nelson Mandela's interminable imprisonment.

There is so much injustice and suffering crying out for our attention: victims of hunger, or racism and political persecution, writers and poets, prisoners in so many lands governed by the left and by the right. Human rights are being violated on every continent. More people are oppressed than free.

Palestinians and Israelis

And then, too, there are the Palestinians to whose plight I am sensitive but whose methods I deplore. Violence and terrorism are not the answer. Something must be done about their suffering, and soon. I trust Israel, for I have faith in the Jewish people. Let Israel be given a chance, let hatred and danger be removed from her horizons, and there will be peace in and around the Holy Land.

Yes, I have faith. Faith in God and even in His creation. Without it no action would be possible. And action is the only remedy to indifference: the most insidious danger of all. Isn't this the

meaning of Alfred Nobel's legacy? Wasn't his fear of war a shield against war?

There is much to be done, there is much that can be done. One person—a Raoul Wallenberg, an Albert Schweitzer, one person of integrity, can make a difference, a difference of life and death. As long as one dissident is in prison, our freedom will not be true. As long as one child is hungry, our lives will be filled with anguish and shame.

What all these victims need above all is to know that they are not alone; that we are not forgetting them, that when their voices are stifled we shall lend them ours, that while their freedom depends on ours, the quality of our freedom depends on theirs.

'Every Hour an Offering'

This is what I say to the young Jewish boy wondering what I have done with his years. It is in his name that I speak to you and that I express to you my deepest gratitude. No one is as capable of gratitude as one who has emerged from the kingdom of night.

We know that every moment is a moment of grace, every hour an offering; not to share them would mean to betray them. Our lives no longer belong to us alone; they belong to all those who need us desperately.

Thank you, Chairman Aarvik. Thank you, members of the Nobel Committee. Thank you, people of Norway, for declaring on this singular occasion that our survival has meaning for mankind.

ELIE WIESEL

TIMELINE

1928	September 30—Born in Sighet, Rumania, to Shlomo and Sarah Wiesel
1944	Taken to Auschwitz concentration camp
1945	Moved to Buchenwald concentration camp
1945	Set free; moved to France
1948-51	Studied at Sorbonne, Paris, France; worked as journalist
1956	Applied for United States citizenship; *And the World Has Remained Silent* published in Buenos Aires
1958	*Night (La Nuit)* published in France
1963	Became a United States citizen
1965	Made first trip to the Soviet Union
1969	Married Marian Erster Rose
1972-76	Taught at City University of New York
1976	Was made Andrew Mellon Professor in the Humanities at Boston University
1978	Was appointed chairman of the United States Holocaust Memorial Council
1985	Received the Congressional Gold Medal of Achievement
1986	Received the Nobel Peace Prize

ABOUT THE AUTHOR

CAROL GREENE has degrees in English Literature and Musicology. She has worked in international exchange programs, as an editor and as a teacher. She now lives in Saint Louis, Missouri, and writes full-time. She has published over fifty books—most of them for children. Other Childrens Press biographies by Ms. Greene include *Sandra Day O'Connor; Mother Teresa*; *Indira Nehru Gandhi*; *Diana, Princess of Wales;* and *Desmond Tutu* in the Picture-Story Biography series, and *Louisa May Alcott, Marie Curie, Thomas Alva Edison, Hans Christian Andersen,* and *Marco Polo* in the People of Distinction series.